GOOGLE YOUR HOME

SETTING UP A NETWORK OF NEST
DEVICES IN YOUR HOME

SCOTT LA COUNTE

ANAHEIM, CALIFORNIA

www.RidiculouslySimpleBooks.com

Copyright © 2019 by Scott La Counte.

All rights reserved. No part of this publication may be reproduced, distributed or transmitted in any form or by any means, including photocopying, recording, or other electronic or mechanical methods, without the prior written permission of the publisher, except in the case of brief quotations embodied in critical reviews and certain other noncommercial uses permitted by copyright law.

Limited Liability / Disclaimer of Warranty. While best efforts have been used in preparing this book, the author and publishers make no representations or warranties of any kind and assume no liabilities of any kind with respect to accuracy or completeness of the content and specifically the author nor publisher shall be held liable or responsible to any person or entity with respect to any loss or incidental r consequential damages caused or alleged to have been caused, directly, or indirectly without limitations, by the information or programs contained herein. Furthermore, readers should be aware that the Internet sites listed in this work may have changed or disappeared. This work is sold with the understanding that the advice inside may not be suitable in every situation.

Trademarks. Where trademarks are used in this book this infers no endorsement or any affiliation with this book. Any trademarks (including, but not limiting to, screenshots) used in this book are solely used for editorial and educational purposes.

Table of Contents

Introduction 7
Nest Learning Thermostats..*9*
   Introduction..9
   Popular Alternatives 10
   What You Need to Know 11
      Installation 11
      How to Use 12
      Nest Sensors 12
      Nest Rebates 13
   Using the Physical Nest 14
   Using the Nest App 21
Nest Cams *33*
   Introduction... 33
   Popular Alternatives 34
   What You Need to Know 35
      Installation 35
   The Nest Cam Crash Course 36
Nest Hello..*49*
   Introduction... 49
   Popular Alternatives 50

What You Need to Know 50
    Installation 50

Nest Hello Crash Course 51

Nest Secure Alarm 60

Introduction 60

Popular Alternatives 61

What you need to know 61
    Installation 61

Nest Secure Alarm Crash Course 62

Nest Protect 72

Introduction 72

Popular Alternatives 72

What You Need To Know 73
    Installation 73

Nest Protect Crash Course 74

Nest WiFi 83

Introduction 83

Popular Alternatives 84

What You Need To Know 84
    Installation 84
    Specs 84
    Unboxing 85

The Setup 87
    Access Point 97

Managing Nest Wifi 106

About the Author..119

Disclaimer: *Please note, while every effort has been made to ensure accuracy, this book is not endorsed by Alphabet, Inc. and should be considered unofficial.*

INTRODUCTION

The smart house has arrived. The days of buying from one company for your home security, another company for your thermostat, and still another for your doorbell camera are behind us!

You can still do that, of course, but today's smart homes can easily belong to one ecosystem, which allows them to interact better with each other.

This book will look at how to make your home "smart" using Google products. It will cover:
- Nest Learning Thermostats
- Nest Cams
- Nest Hello (Doorbell Camera)
- Nest Secure Alarm
- Nest Protect
- Nest Wifi

This book will not cover Google smart speakers (such as the Google Home and Nest Mini); these devices use Google Assistant, but there's not a lot of settings you need to know about. That said, they do work very well in your home if you have other

Google devices. For example, if you have the Nest Doorbell, your speakers will chime and tell you who is at the door if you have speakers throughout your house. Nest Mini speakers are frequently on sale for less than $30.

This book is based off of iOS, but the Android OS version of Nest is nearly identical.

If you are ready to connect your home to the future, then let's get started.

[1]
NEST LEARNING THERMOSTATS

INTRODUCTION

When you think about the "smart" home, it really all starts with the thermostats. Smart thermostats allow you to adjust the feel of the home—right in the palm of your hand.

You can tell it to change to a certain temperature when you leave work or come home. Adjust it so certain rooms cool to different temperatures. And so much more.

When it comes to smart thermostats, Nest is the one who really started it all. Others were doing it—or thinking about doing it—but Nest was the one who became a household name.

Popular Alternatives

- Honeywell WiFi 7-Day Programmable Thermostat (approx. $79.99); syncs to voice activated devices like Alexa as well as smartphones, so you can control the temperature from your phone.
- Vine Wifi Programmable Thermostat (approx. $85); all the standard features of a Wifi thermostat (notably remote controlled from a smartphone), this device also boasts a color screen, night light, and a built-in weather forecaster.
- Honeywell Smart Color Programmable Thermostat (approx. $199); if you want the Honeywell system and don't mind paying more for a color screen and touch screen, then this is the system for you. It has a smart technology built in that can help learn your preferences in a way similar to the Nest.

What You Need to Know

Nest was cutting edge in smart thermostats when it first came out in 2011; over the years, it's remained the leader that other companies follow. They tend to invent the features and other companies tend to copy them. It's also built a reputation as an energy saver; the energy company in my area offers a yearly rewards program if you use your Nest alongside their service. There's nothing extra to do. You just have to agree to your Nest to turn off at certain times to save on energy. While the Nest is more than many other thermostats, this alone has paid for the device a few times over. I recommend seeing if your county offers something similar.

Installation

All Nest products are easy to install, but if you aren't comfortable with electrical work, this is one system that's better left to the pros. Many companies will bundle a free installation with their service. For example, my alarm service came out and did a free install; I just had to buy the unit. There were no extra contracts to sign and it did not extend the service I had with the company.

How to Use

I am not covering the installation of a Nest Thermostat. While it is possible to install yourself (and there are plenty of videos online to walk you through it), I personally believe it is better to let a pro do it unless you are comfortable working around electricity.

Nest Sensors

I've included examples of using the Nest Temperature Sensors, so my screenshots may look different than yours. The problem some have with Nest is the sensor is located in a hallway that is cooler than anywhere else in your room; adding sensors lets your Nest see the temperature in other rooms and adjust accordingly; for example, you can say, use the bedrooms temperature instead of the hallways. The sensors cost approximately $39 each. Unlike the Nest Thermostat, the Nest Sensors are very easy to install. They stick on the wall with no wires.

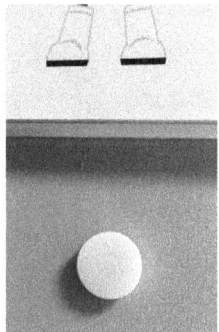

To add a sensor, you go into the Nest app, tap the config in the upper right corner, and tap Add Product, then follow the instructions. It's very quick and painless to install.

NEST REBATES

I also recommend seeing if rebates are available for using your thermostat. To check, open the Nest app, tap the config button in the upper right corner, then tap Rebates and rewards.

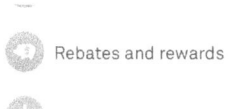

If you are enrolled in any programs, you will see it here. If you don't see anything you can tap Nest Rebates and Rewards at the bottom of the screen.

14 | *Google Your Home*

This will launch a website that lets you search by zip code for rewards.

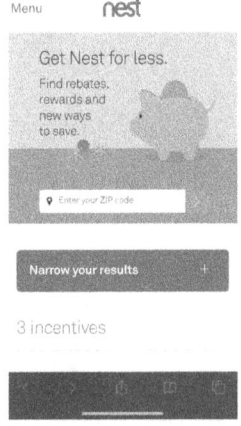

USING THE PHYSICAL NEST

Almost anything you can adjust on your phone or tablet can also be adjusted on the device. Most people will probably find it's easier to do on their phone or tablet, but there might be instances where your app isn't available so it's good to know how to do both.

The physical device is very easy to use; turn it like a dial to move to different icons and options; push the device in to select the icon or option.

When you pass by the Nest, it will automatically sense your presence and light up; it will tell you if it's currently on and what the thermostat is set to.

Push the device in one time, and all of the options will come up. I'll cover each option going from upper left to right.

16 | *Google Your Home*

The first option lets you pick the mode: Heat, Cool, or Heat / Cool. Once you make your selection, you can adjust the thermostat to the temperature that you want.

The leaf will start eco mode, which will adjust when your Nest turns on to help you save energy.

Scott La Counte | 17

If you have sensors installed, you can use the next option to pick what sensor you want to use.

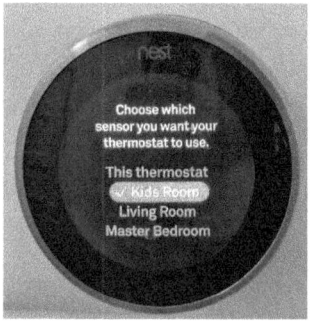

The next setting will turn your fan on; your thermostat must be on for this to work.

The Nest allows you to set schedules for when you want it to turn on. To use, go to the day / time you want and push the Nest in.

Next, select New by pushing in on the device.

You can go to the scheduled day, and push it again to remove it or change it.

The history will tell you how much heat and air you have used for a particular day.

Finally, the settings let you dial through all the possible settings that you can change.

The following settings are available (most of these can be more easily changed in the app, but there are a few you'll only find on the device—Nest Pro, for example, which is a setting an installer may use).

- Home / Away
- Eco
- Safety temperature
- Sensor schedule
- Fan schedule
- Nest Sense
- Reminders
- Energy programs
- Nest Protect
- Display
- Brightness
- Click sound

- F / C
- Date & time
- Language
- Nest app
- Location
- Network
- Lock
- Placement
- Equipment
- Nest Pro
- Software
- Technical info
- Legal info
- Reset

Using the Nest App

This section is going to cover the mobile app; I am using an iPhone in the examples, but the UI is very similar on Android and iPadOS—things are laid out a little differently because of different sizes and orientations, but all the features / settings are there.

If you are away from your mobile device, you can also access Nest by going to Nest.com and logging into your account. Again, it looks slightly different, but all the same settings and features are there.

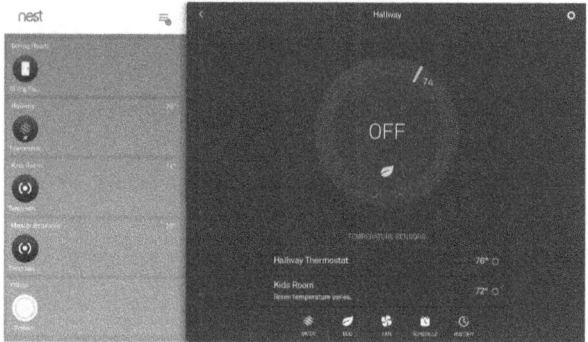

When you open the Nest app, you can access your thermostat by tapping on either the icon for the Nest device (see below under Hallway) or the sensor if you have installed one (see below under Kids Room).

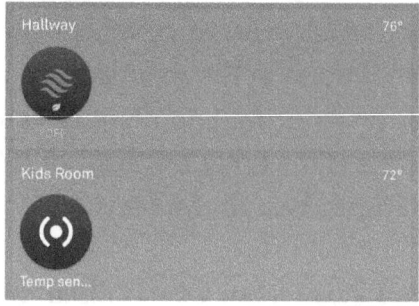

Either option takes you to the same screen.

On this screen, you can select the sensor you want to use (just tap on the room and it will switch).

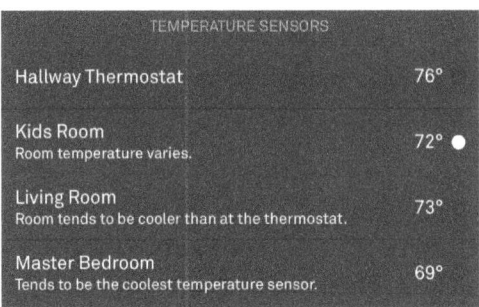

Scroll down a little and you can see the humidity level and outside temperature.

24 | *Google Your Home*

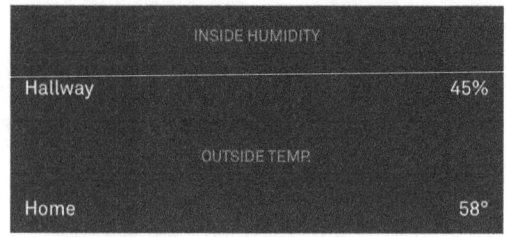

At the bottom are icons for Mode, Eco, Fan, Schedule, and History.

Mode lets you select the mode you want to use: Heat, Cool, Heat / Cool or Off.

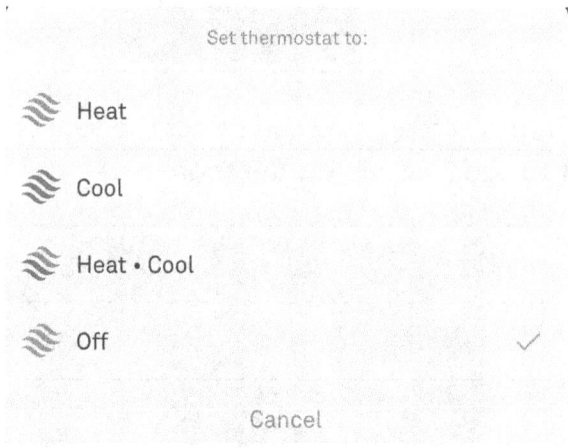

Eco lets you turn on an energy-saving mode.

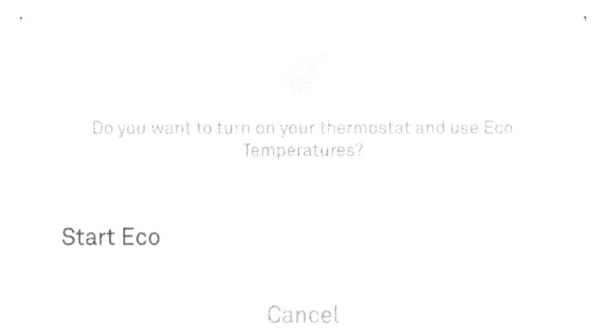

Fan turns on the fan (but you must first have the thermostat on).

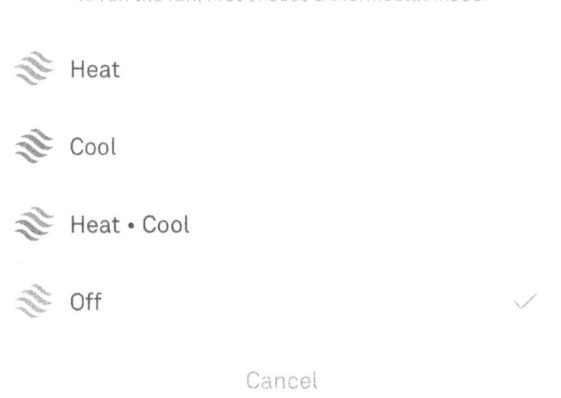

Schedule lets you program in a schedule to turn on cooling or heating.

26 | *Google Your Home*

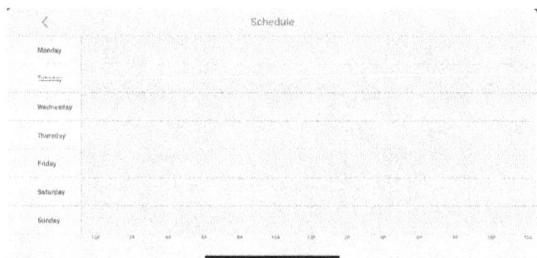

To use it, just tap on the date / time range; this will zoom in slightly and give you an Add option in the lower right corner. Tapping it once more and tapping Remove will remove it.

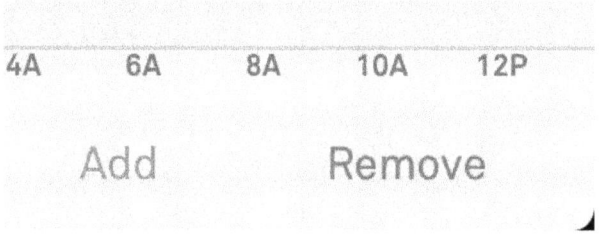

Finally, Energy History will give you a report of how often you have used heat or air over a period of time.

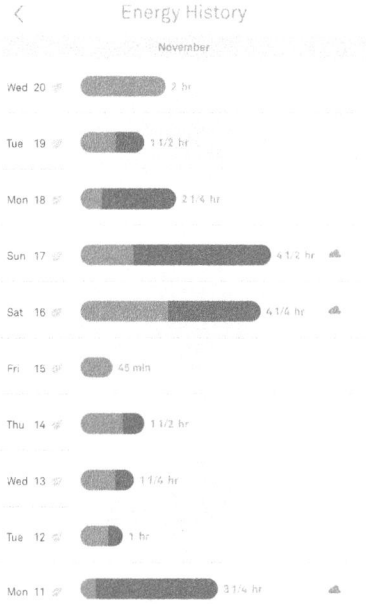

In the upper right corner of the main screen, you can tap the config icon to go into your device settings.

Most of the settings are just toggles; some won't apply to your home; some settings don't even have settings—they're more of an FYI.

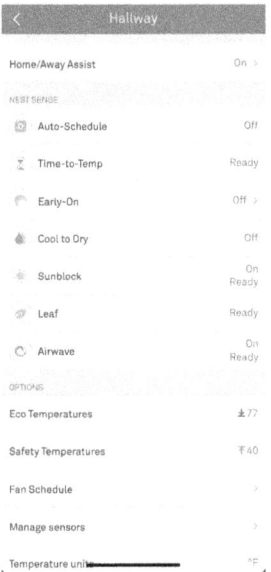

Home / Away Assist is a setting that goes on automatically when you are away; if you have a Nest security system, this works when you set the alarm to away. You can decide how cool the house should be when you are away.

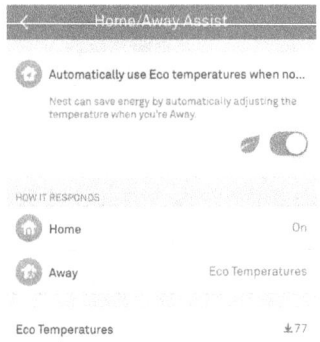

Auto-Schedule learns about when you turn your system on and off—basically your habits—and starts to create an energy-saving schedule around it.

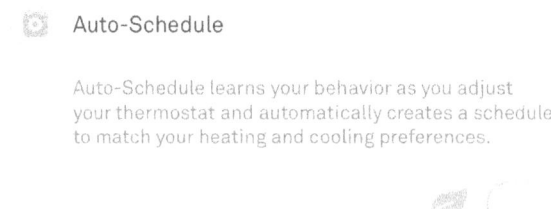

Early-On is another energy-saving feature that helps you reach your desired temperature at a more gradual pace.

Cool to Dry is a humidity feature, but notice the disclaimer below: it can be expensive. Depending on where you live, you may find your energy bill increasing because it is turned on.

Cool to Dry

Cool to Dry reduces excessive indoor humidity using your air conditioner. Lowering indoor humidity can be healthier for your place.

This can be expensive: Cool to Dry may cool beyond the temperature you set.

Sunblock cools your home when it detects the sun coming in.

 Sunblock

Sunblock tells Nest when it's in direct sunlight so it can adjust the temperature correctly.

Airwave uses both your fan and your air to help keep a room cool and save energy and costs.

 Airwave

Airwave automatically switches off your air-conditioner compressor after the room has cooled. It uses the fan to spread the remaining cool air throughout your place, saving cooling costs.

The next set of features will be less frequently used—you might set them once and then never use them again. Temperature units just changes the measurement; Eco Temperatures is just the temperature you want Eco mode to be at.

OPTIONS

Eco Temperatures   77

Safety Temperatures   40

Fan Schedule   >

Manage sensors   >

Temperature units   °F

Wi-Fi connection

Finally, the About section is something you will probably only use if there's a problem and you need to talk to support. They might ask you things like what is the model number (which is under Equipment).

ABOUT	
Where	Hallway >
Equipment	>
Technical info	
Your Data	>
NEST TEMPERATURE SENSORS	
Kids Room	>
Living Room	>
Master Bedroom	>

Remove thermostat

[2]
NEST CAMS

INTRODUCTION

The idea of having cameras in every room used to be only for businesses. Cameras have officially entered the home and they have so many purposes.

While security is certainly on the mind of most people when they buy a camera, the nursery is probably in close second.

Nest Cams aren't just cameras—they're smart cameras. They can detect when something is a dog vs when it's someone talking. They can recognize faces. And they can store all of this in the Cloud.

Popular Alternatives

- Logitech Circle 2 (approx. $180); boasts a wide-angle lens to capture even more, and two-way audio detection.
- Amazon Cloud Cam (approx. $120); ideal if you are on the Amazon ecosystem, as it will show up on your Echo Show; will notify you if it detects sounds like smoke alarms or glass breaking.
- Ring Stick Up Cam (approx. $150); Ring is now owned by Amazon, which means it ties into Amazon's ecosystem well; it also has an optional rechargeable battery, which makes it ideal for people who want a security camera outside but don't want to put down wiring.
- Wyze Cam (approx. $26); if you want simple without all the bells and whistles, then Wyze is definitely one of the best budget cameras out there; not only does it have a very affordable price, but it has 14 days of free cloud storage.

What You Need to Know

Nest Cams tend to be more bandwidth hogs. They can record at very sharp resolutions, and store days' worth of footage. If you have an Internet provider with a slow speed, this can be problematic. Nest also has Nest Aware as an add-on. Currently it's $50 a year for the first year and $30 for each additional camera. That gives you even more features—like extended cloud recording history and the ability to see who is at the door (Is it a dog walking by? A person talking? Or a face that it recognizes?). Remember that there is an indoor and outdoor version of this device. They work essentially the same, but the outdoor can withstand the elements that outdoors bring.

Installation

One of the easier products to install. Unlike other Nest products, you don't need any advanced electrical skillset (unless you are plugging it in outside) and will probably have no problem installing it yourself.

The Nest Cam Crash Course

This guide will cover Nest Cams with Nest Aware on; Nest Aware is a paid add-on; subscription prices vary, and it includes multi-day recording, 24/7 cloud recording, activity zones, and intelligent alerts (meaning it can detect things like dogs barking vs. people shouting), and more. Nest cameras work perfectly fine without the add-on, but personally I think the add-ons are well worth the price. A trial is included with your camera so you can judge for yourself.

If you decide to not buy Nest Aware, then this guide will still make sense; there will just be a few features that you don't see.

It should also be noted that there are different kinds of Nest cameras (Nest Cam IQ and Nest Cam Outdoor); this section is covering the base camera, but if you own the other cameras, these features should still be there—the other cameras behave almost identically to the Nest Cam.

To get started, go to your Nest app, then tap on the preview of your camera.

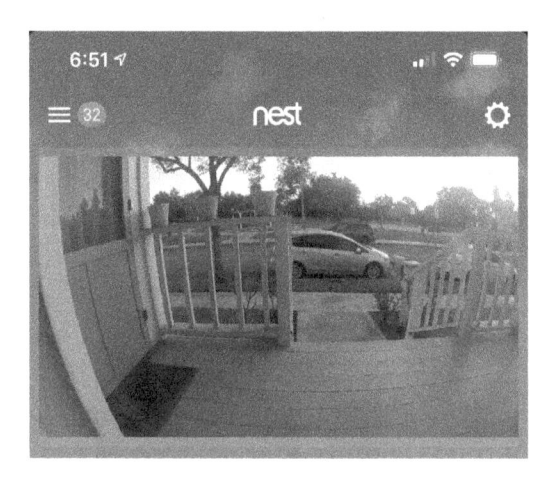

This brings up a live view of your camera with the history.

You can see a full screen view of your camera by tapping on the down arrow under the video.

Tap the up arrow to return to normal view; at any point you can also pinch to zoom in and out.

The history, by default, will show everything; if you only want to see the sequences when it detected some kind of activity, tap the three lines to the right of the arrow.

This will group all your events together so it's a little easier to see.

At the bottom of your screen is the tab menu; you can see your history by tapping on the calendar icon. If you'd like to use your camera's microphone to talk to someone you see in the clip, tap Talk (you'll hear a chime on the camera when you do this); finally you can create a video clip with the last option.

To get into your camera's settings, tap the video feed one time, then tap the config icon in the upper right corner (you can also use this action to go backwards or forwards in your video feed by 15-second intervals).

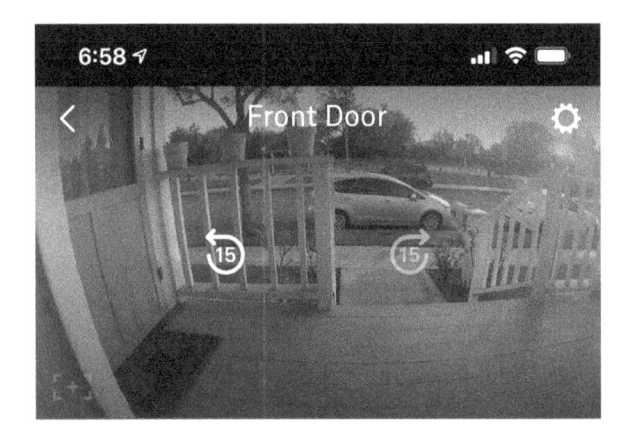

The camera settings are camera specific—meaning what you see here only applies to the current camera—not all of the cameras.

Camera On/Off	
Home/Away Assist	Off >
Schedule	Off >
Notifications	>
Activity Zones	>
Nest Aware	>
VIDEO	
Quality and bandwidth	HIGH
Night Vision	Off
Rotate image	Off
Camera sharing	Not shared
DEVICE OPTIONS	
Status light	AUTO >
Microphone	>

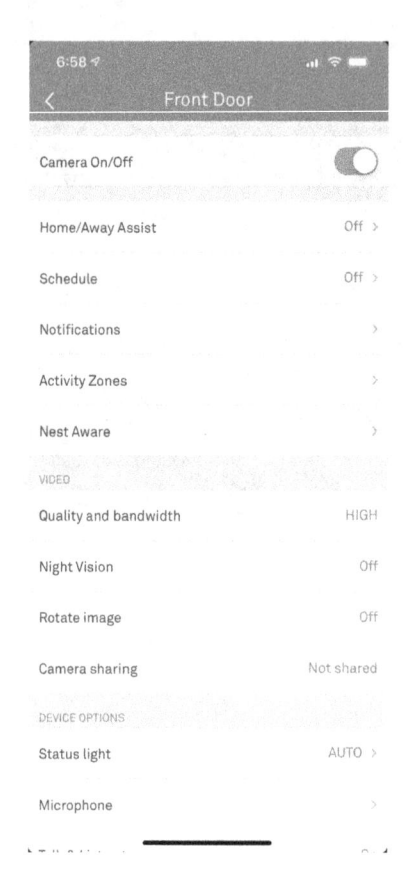

    Most of the settings are pretty self-explanatory; Activity Zones is a very useful setting for capturing people on your camera. One of my cameras, for example, is on my porch; I don't need to get an alert every time someone walks in front of my house; I just want to know when someone walks on my porch; so I have a zone that says "only run activity alerts if a person is within the defined areas."

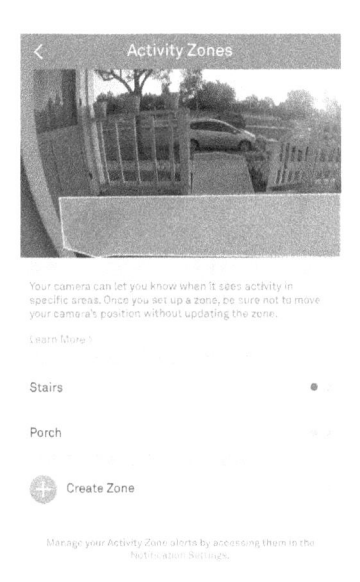

To create a zone, tap the Create Zone option near the bottom of your screen. This will let you drag a box over the video; drag the corners to adjust the range. You can use colors to help you visually see the box. You can also name your zone. That way your alert will tell you exactly what zone was triggered and it makes sense—if I get an alert saying a person was spotted in Zone 3, I'll have to think about what area I set up as Zone 3; naming it just makes it a little easier to remember.

The Video section lets you adjust how a video is recorded.

VIDEO	
Quality and bandwidth	HIGH
Night Vision	Off
Rotate image	Off
Camera sharing	Not shared

I have my quality set to the highest settings because my Internet provider doesn't throttle or cap my uses; if your provider does, then you might want to consider lowering this setting. The Nest Cam is higher than most cameras because it is recording everything.

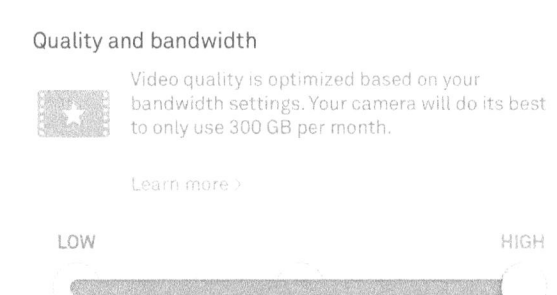

Quality and bandwidth

Video quality is optimized based on your bandwidth settings. Your camera will do its best to only use 300 GB per month.

Learn more

LOW   HIGH

Your internet provider may limit your bandwidth usage or charge you extra if you use too much.

Night Vision adjusts the camera when it is in low light settings (i.e. night); I have this setting turned off because I have a motion light on my porch that illuminates the area; I personally don't like the infrared light that comes on to record the area in low light.

Night Vision

Night Vision lets you keep an eye on things, in low light and in the dark. Video will be in black and white whenever Night Vision is on.

OFF   AUTO   ALWAYS ON

DEFAULT

Camera sharing lets you add other people to your Nest account to see your camera; this is done online at home.nest.com.

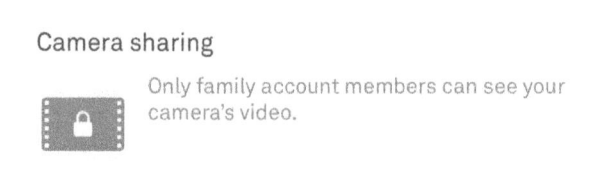

Camera sharing

Only family account members can see your camera's video.

The home's owner can change this setting at home.nest.com.

The Device Options are the features available to the device.

DEVICE OPTIONS

Status light	AUTO >
Microphone	>
Talk & Listen tone	On
Wi-Fi connection	

The Status light is the little green light above the camera that lets people know it's on; you can set it to low if you find it distracting.

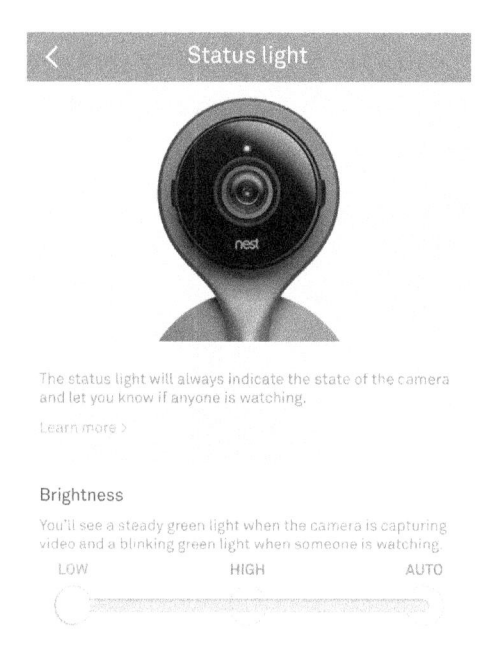

> **Status light**
>
> The status light will always indicate the state of the camera and let you know if anyone is watching.
>
> Learn more >
>
> **Brightness**
> You'll see a steady green light when the camera is capturing video and a blinking green light when someone is watching.
>
> LOW   HIGH   AUTO

About lets you change the location of the Nest and see technical information that might be asked for if you contact support.

> ABOUT
>
> Where   Front Door >
>
> Technical info
>
> Your Data   >

Finally, at the bottom of your settings is the option to delete your video history and remove your camera (removing the camera takes it out of your Nest account).

Delete video history

Remove camera

[3]
NEST HELLO

INTRODUCTION

Ring may have taken the doorbell into the modern age, but Nest Hello is a worthy competitor and beats it on many different levels.

The main selling point for Nest Hello is it's always on recording—it doesn't activate only when someone pushes the button. Nest also has Nest Aware, which detects people, voices, and more.

Popular Alternatives

- Eufy (approx. $150); boost customizable responses, an add-on wireless chime, and local storage.
- Ring Video Doorbell (approx. $99); Ring is perhaps the best option for those who want a rechargeable system that you can install with zero wiring—but that comes at a price: the video quality usually isn't as good and it doesn't record 24/7; Ring also ties in well to Amazon's ecosystem. Finally, Ring has a social network built into the app, so neighbors can report crime, stolen packages and more with their fellow neighbors.

What You Need to Know

Nest Hello records everything: 24/7. That means it's a bandwidth hog. This is why it requires an electrical connection. You can adjust the resolution of the recordings, which helps, but if you have slower Internet, it still becomes problematic.

Installation

Installation usually requires a professional. You can do it yourself, but you should be comfortable working with electrical wires. Unlike most doorbell cams, Nest Hello needs to use your internal doorbell chime—there are no wireless add-ons. Personally, my chime is broken, but the Nest rings on Google Nest Home devices, so it's not really essential—even though it's technically required.

Nest Hello Crash Course

The Nest Hello is essentially a Nest Cam with a button on it. That means if you know how to use the Nest Cam, then this is going to be a breeze. In this section, I will go over some of the added features, but I won't go into details about things covered in the previous section.

You can tell the difference between a Nest Cam and Nest Hello by the size of the video; Nest Hello is more square and Nest Cam is more rectangular. Tapping on the screen pulls up the live view.

Once you get into the live view, things look almost identical.

The biggest difference is at the bottom of the screen: there are five options instead of three.

| 5 DAYS | PEOPLE | TALK | NEW CLIP | QUIET TIME |

The first option lets you pull up a history of your recordings.

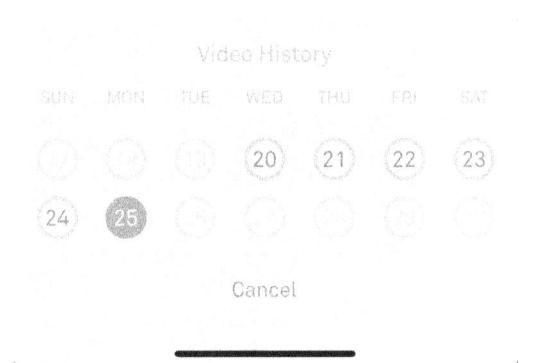

People shows you people that it has detected (if any); these are only new people—if you have stored people, then it won't show them again.

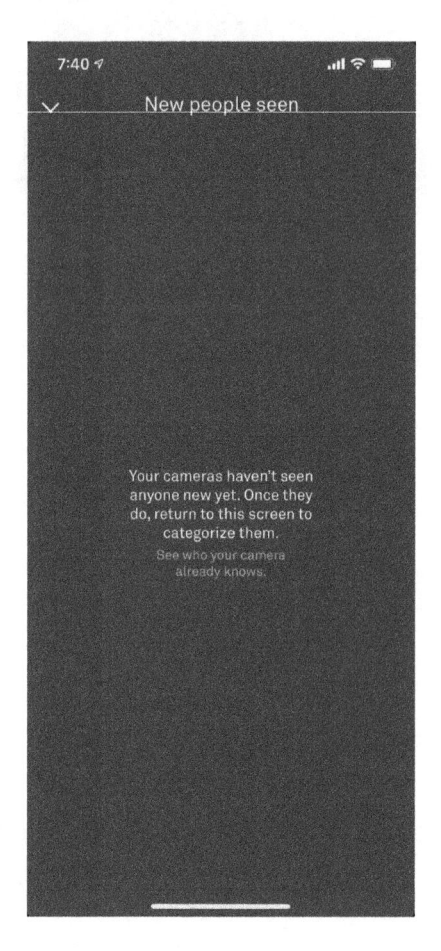

Quiet time lets you mute your chime for a period of time—it does still record, however.

The settings menu also looks very similar to the Nest Cam, but there are a few additional settings. There's a new setting, for example, to turn the inside chime On / Off.

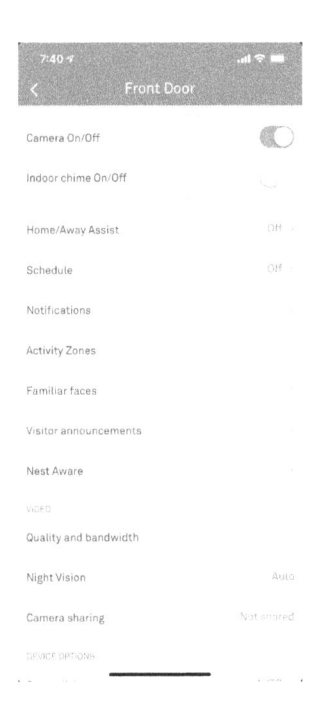

One of the really stand out features of Nest Hello is under Familiar faces; this is a facial recognition feature that helps you know who is at the door. For example, I have set mine up to detect different package carriers (i.e. UPS, USPS, FedEx, etc.), so when they ring the doorbell my Google

Home will announce that it's UPS or whoever it detects. As you get started, it will probably detect the person multiple times; you can use the Select button in the upper right corner to merge them together into one. Also, notice I said "My Google Home"? This is another example of how Google works well with other Google products.

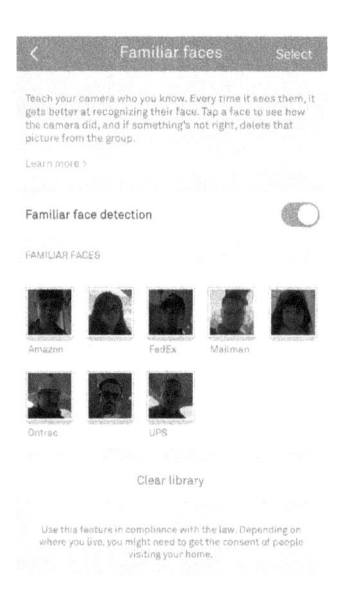

When someone rings the doorbell that it doesn't detect, it will show up as an alert on this screen. You can tap it to see who it is, and (if you want) add them to facial recognition.

Clear library

Use this feature in compliance with the law. Depending on where you live, you might need to get the consent of people visiting your home.

> Your camera saw someone new. Tap to see who it is.

You'll see a screen that shows you a picture and it will ask you if you know them; select Yes to add them.

Device Options also has a few extra features.

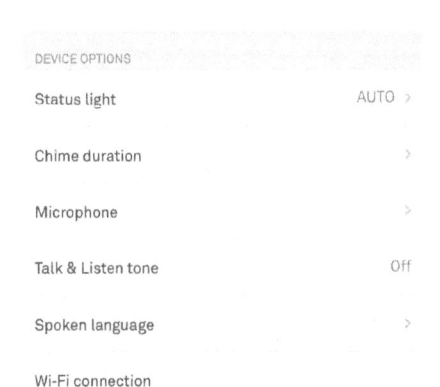

DEVICE OPTIONS	
Status light	AUTO >
Chime duration	>
Microphone	>
Talk & Listen tone	Off
Spoken language	>
Wi-Fi connection	

Chime duration is a simple toggle switch; if you want to adjust it, toggle it on.

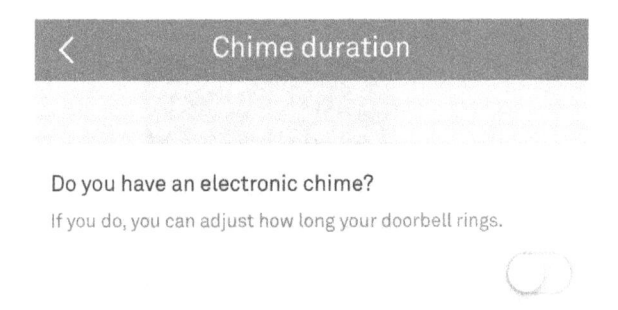

< Chime duration

Do you have an electronic chime?
If you do, you can adjust how long your doorbell rings.

Then make your adjustment.

< Chime duration

Do you have an electronic chime?
If you do, you can adjust how long your doorbell rings.

Chime duration
1 sec

Nest Hello can make announcements to the person at the door when they push the doorbell; Spoken language lets you pick what language this announcement is in.

[4]
Nest Secure Alarm

Introduction

I remember my first security system. First there was a consultation. Then contracts. Then a guy who spent several hours in the house setting it up.

Today, security systems are becoming much more DIY. You don't need a professional installer, and you certainly don't need contracts that lock you into that provider for months or even years.

Better yet, you can take your alarm system with you pretty easily.

Popular Alternatives

Security systems used to cost a fortune—and then you had to get someone to monitor it after the install. Today, a number of companies offer DIY solutions. You still can get professional monitoring, but this is not always a requirement. Ring Alarm Security Kit (approx. $199) is the most popular option for anyone wanting to stay in the Amazon Alexa ecosystem. SimpliSafe ($229) pioneered the idea of DIY home security.

What you need to know

Most DIY alarm systems come in bundles; so when you see "approx. $199" above, that's just the starting price. The cost goes up depending on your needs.

Installation

One of the easiest security systems you will ever install. No wiring required. Scan each product and follow the instructions. It's that simple.

Nest Secure Alarm Crash Course

The Nest Secure is a powerful, but minimal system. $399 gets you a very small box! It comes with one Nest Guard (the keypad that turns the alarm off), two Detect Sensors (which double as door alarms), and two Nest Tags (keychain fobs that turn off the alarm when you swipe them over the guard).

Minimal as it is, it's still quite powerful; everything doubles as something else. The Nest Guard is the keypad, but it's also the sensor that detects motion; that's also true with the door alarms (or Detect Sensors). That said, you'll probably want more than three sensors unless you have a small house. You can add Detect Sensors for approximately $49 each; you can only have one Nest Guard. For about $19, you can purchase a Nest sign for your front yard.

The Detect Sensors are very small (about three inches long) and stick onto the surface with adhesive, so they're easy to install.

You can mount them horizontally.

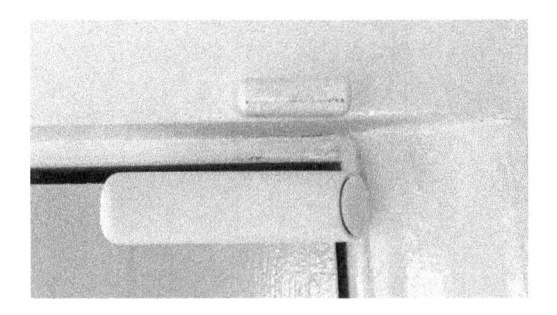

Or vertically.

There's a button on the sensor that disables it. So if you have your alarm on, but need to let the dog out, just press the button and it disables it for a few seconds. You don't have to use it on doors. You can use it anywhere in your house. Corners will usually get the best detect range.

From inside the app, you have two options for managing your alarm system. First is the quick access. That's at the top of the app and says Home.

This is the best access for turning your alarm on and off. Tap it once to turn it on or off.

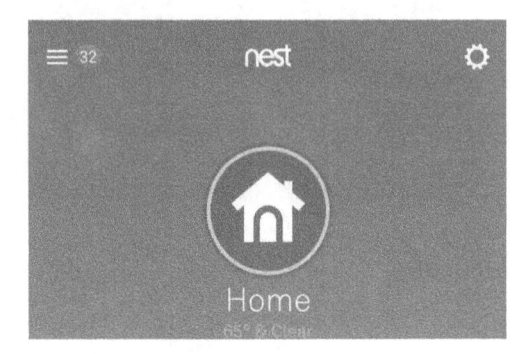

Next, tap Away to turn it on.

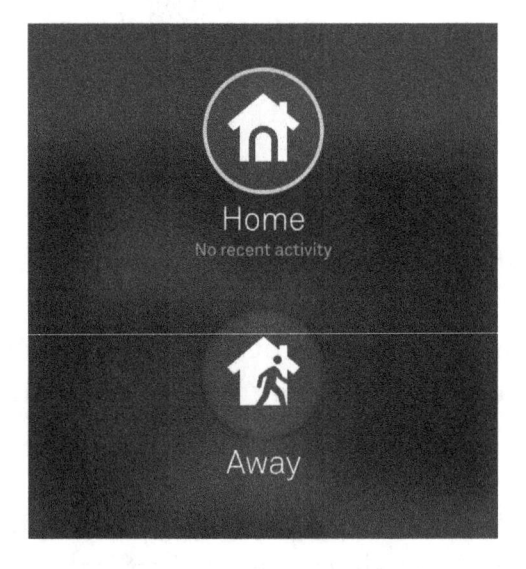

Tap the config icon in the upper right corner, and you can tell your alarm what happens when the

Alarm turns on; for example, do you want a camera to record everything? Do you want the Thermostat to automatically turn off or set to a certain temperature?

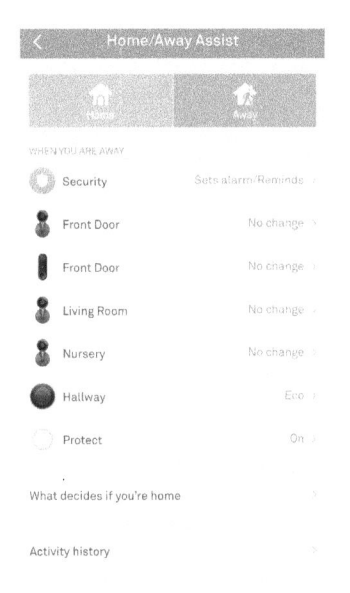

What "defines" Away? Tap the section at the bottom of the screen to tell it. You can select which products will help Nest decide if you are "Away." That way if you forget to turn it on, Nest will send you a notification reminding you that you should turn it on.

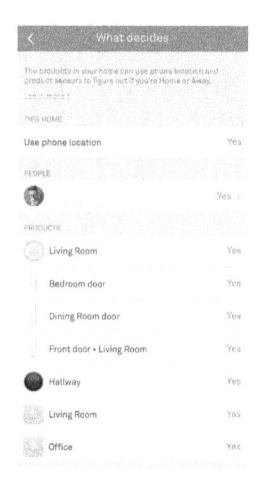

The second option for managing the alarm has more options. It's in the row of icons with all of your devices and says "Guard" under it.

When you tap that, it will give you a third option for arming your system. Notice the three badges? The middle one is to arm the system to Stay; that means you are home, but you want the door alarms on. If you set it to the last option, it will go off if it detects motion, so if you walk to the bathroom in the middle of the night, for example.

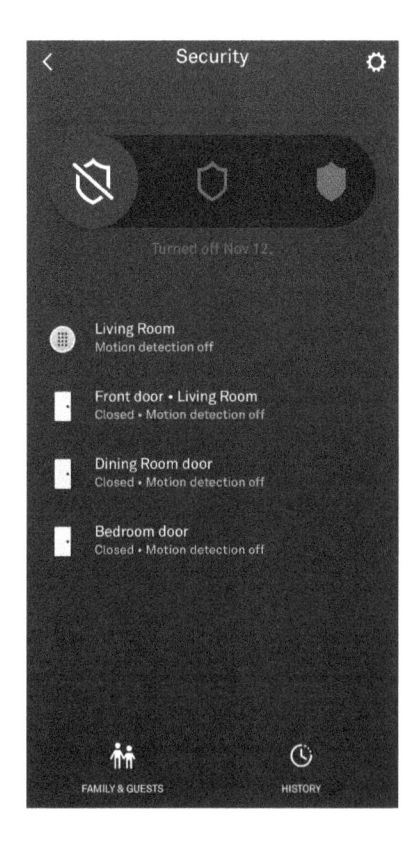

The bottom of the app has two options: Family & Friends and History. Family & Friends lets you add different people who can turn your alarm on and off.

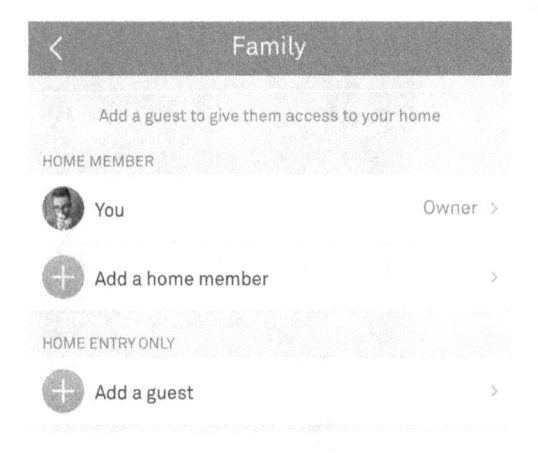

History gives you all the events that have happened in your house.

Tapping on a specific day will give you a detailed list of events; more than likely, it will just be a bunch of doors opening and shutting.

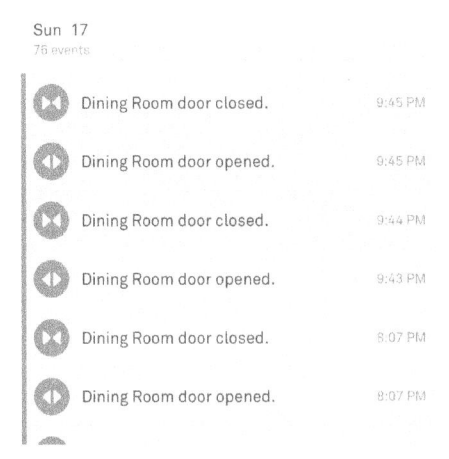

Sun 17		
76 events		
⊗ Dining Room door closed.		9:45 PM
◐ Dining Room door opened.		9:45 PM
⊗ Dining Room door closed.		9:44 PM
◐ Dining Room door opened.		9:43 PM
⊗ Dining Room door closed.		8:07 PM
◐ Dining Room door opened.		8:07 PM

If you tap on the config button in the upper right corner, you'll get into your security system settings.

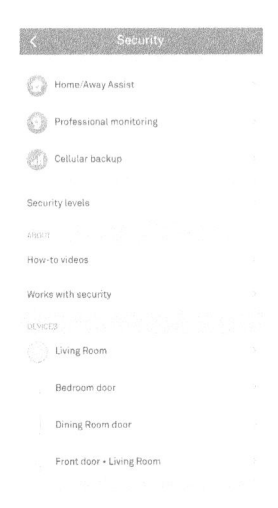

Home / Away Assist is where you'll find most of the settings.

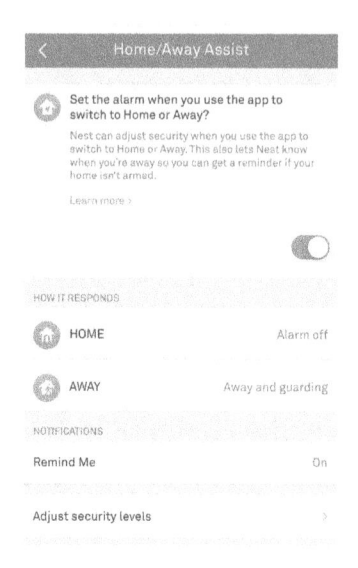

> **Home/Away Assist**
>
> Set the alarm when you use the app to switch to Home or Away?
>
> Nest can adjust security when you use the app to switch to Home or Away. This also lets Nest know when you're away so you can get a reminder if your home isn't armed.
>
> Learn more
>
> HOW IT RESPONDS
>
> HOME — Alarm off
>
> AWAY — Away and guarding
>
> NOTIFICATIONS
>
> Remind Me — On
>
> Adjust security levels

If you are having problems with the alarm being too sensitive to motion (or not sensitive enough), you can tap the Adjust security levels to adjust it. In this area, there's also a section called "Open tones"; that means when you open a door, the Sensor makes a noise. It might be helpful on a door that isn't opened a lot, but for most doors, you may find that it drains the battery of the sensor.

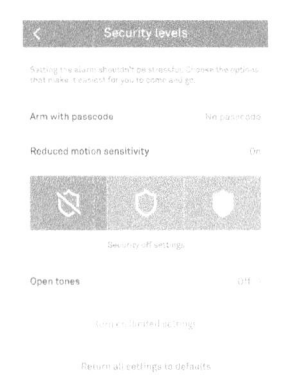

On the main settings screen, you can tap on any of your devices to check the motion range and perform other tests.

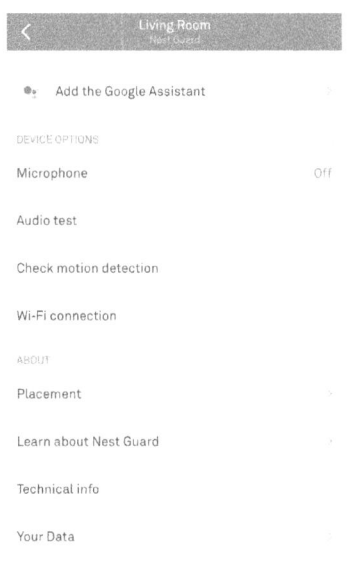

[5]
Nest Protect

Introduction

Fire alarms are great...if you are home! The Nest Protect protects you even when you aren't in the house. And it can notify emergency personal as well. What's more, the systems talk to each other and all connect to each other.

Popular Alternatives

- Onelink Safe & Sound Smart Smoke + Carbon Monoxide Alarm (approx.

$249.99) - This alarm system doubles as a smart speaker with Amazon Alexa inside.
- One of the cheapest alternatives to having a smart alarm is installing what's called a Listener (Ring has one for approx. $35); a listener is placed near a smoke alarm and sends you alerts when it hears it go off.

What You Need To Know

Nests are battery operated. You can also hard wire them so you won't have to replace the batteries, but this will require knowledge of wiring. Make sure and buy Nest Protects in bundles, so you'll save a little bit of money.

Installation

If you are comfortable being on a ladder and using a power drill, then you'll find nothing difficult about this installation. If you'd rather not install it, you might consider getting a handyman to do the mounting and leave you with the software installation—which is nothing more than scanning the devices and following instructions.

Nest Protect Crash Course

There's not a lot to the Nest Protect. Like most of the Nest products, you use the Nest app to add the device, then follow the very simple walkthrough. Setup should take no more than 10 to 15 minutes.

Once it is installed, there are a few things you can do in the app, but they're mostly small settings you'll adjust once and then never again. The main purpose of the app for Nest Protect is to tell you everything is working fine and you are safe.

That said, let's walk through the few Nest Protect settings that you can fix.

From the Nest app, you'll find the Nest Protect in the row of icons; it should have a green circle—if it's red or orange that means there's a problem with the Nest Protect. Tap it one time to go into the settings (if there's a problem, tapping it will also show you what's going on).

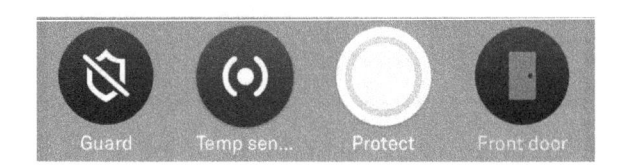

The app will show you an in-app notification about the status of the alarm.

Tapping See History will show you previous checks on the device.

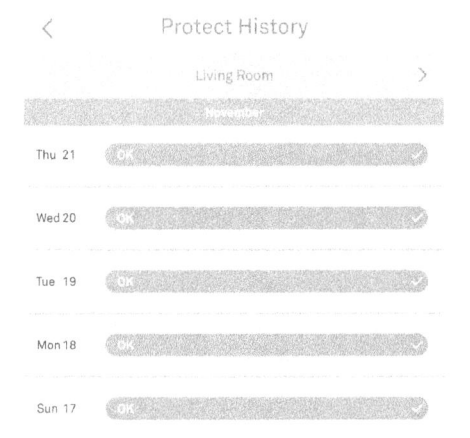

The main Nest Protect screen doesn't have many options. Tapping on any of your Nest Protects under Every is OK will just show the same notification.

The bottom row has two options: Checkup and History. Tapping on history shows the same History previously seen in the notification.

Tapping on checkup will give you information about the last checkup and tell you how to perform a new one.

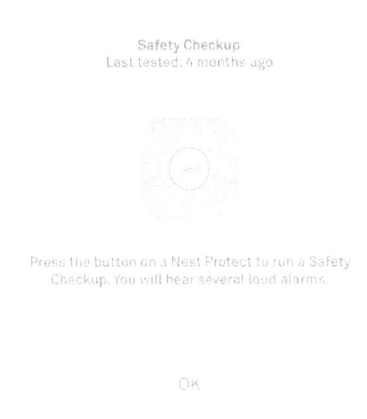

Safety Checkup
Last tested: 4 months ago

Press the button on a Nest Protect to run a Safety Checkup. You will hear several loud alarms.

OK

If you tap on the config button in the upper right corner, you'll go into the Nest Protect settings.

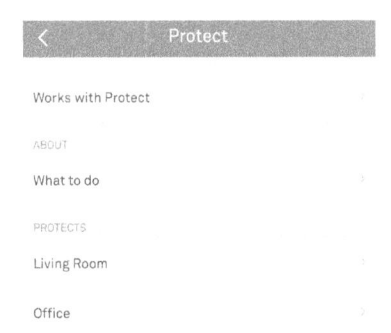

<	Protect	
Works with Protect		
ABOUT		
What to do		
PROTECTS		
Living Room		
Office		

Works with Protect will show you what other Nest devices you have that will interact with the alarm. The cameras, for example, can record smoke if detected.

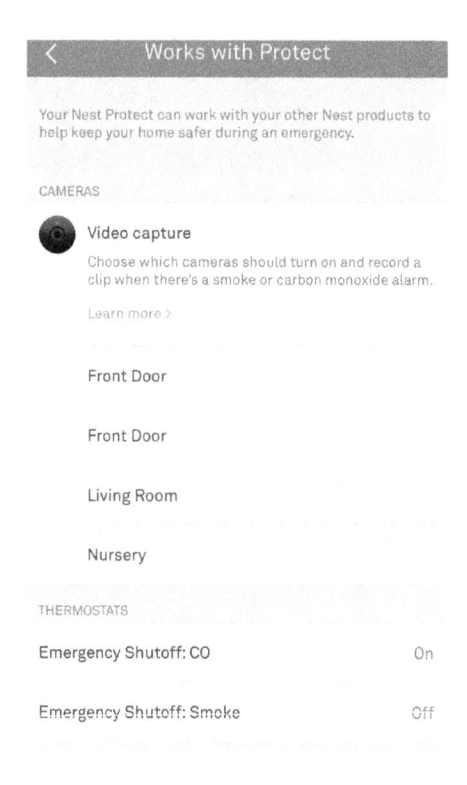

> **Works with Protect**
>
> Your Nest Protect can work with your other Nest products to help keep your home safer during an emergency.
>
> CAMERAS
>
> Video capture
> Choose which cameras should turn on and record a clip when there's a smoke or carbon monoxide alarm.
> Learn more >
>
> Front Door
>
> Front Door
>
> Living Room
>
> Nursery
>
> THERMOSTATS
>
> Emergency Shutoff: CO   On
>
> Emergency Shutoff: Smoke   Off

What to Do is just a few tips about what to do during fires and other emergencies.

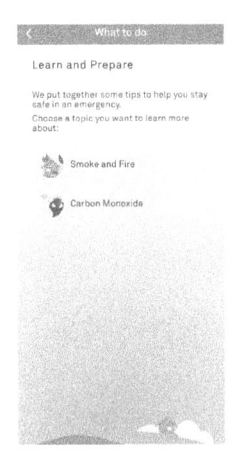

If you tap on any of your devices, you'll get settings specific to that device. These are mostly just on / off toggles.

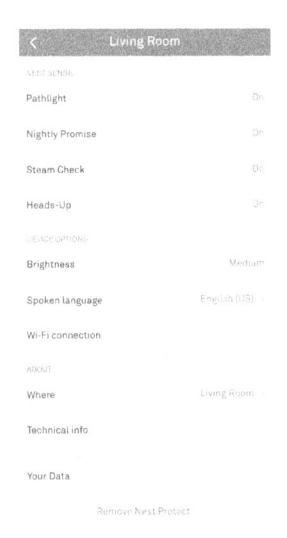

Your Nest Protect can function as a pathlight; when you walk under it, it automatically lights up—it's not bright—just bright enough to show the area in the general space under it.

Pathlight

Pathlight guides your way when the room is dark.

It can turn on for a moment when someone walks by.

Nightly Promise will show you a green indicator when you turn out the lights to remind you the Nest is there protecting you; if it's any color other than green, then there's a problem. Usually the problem is a low battery.

Nightly Promise

Nest Protect lets you know it is working by glowing green for a moment when you turn out the lights.

Nest Protect will glow yellow if there is a problem, even if you turn off Nightly Promise.

Steam Check is for those people who love hot showers. It helps the Nest Protect know if the smoke it detects is just steam.

Steam Check

A nice hot shower should be relaxing, not annoying. Steam Check cuts down on false alarms from steam.

Heads-Up is an early warning feature. If you are prone to burning things in the kitchen like me, then you'll love this feature! It gives you a softer warning and gives you time to open a few windows before the loud blaring goes off.

Heads-Up

Heads-Up lets you know in advance of an alarm that smoke or carbon monoxide levels are rising. And it's not as loud.

Brightness is how bright the pathlight is. I recommend the medium or low setting to save battery life.

Brightness

How bright would you like the Pathlight and Nightly Promise for this Nest Protect?

LOW   MEDIUM   HIGH

Changes may affect battery life.

The other settings are about placement and tech data that you probably will never use unless you contact tech support.

[6]
NEST WIFI

INTRODUCTION

Wi-Fi has always been problematic. Yes, it's amazing when you are in the room with the router. But what about upstairs, in the room in the far corner, or the house with cement walls?

Nest Wifi is a lifesaver for many homes by offering you whole-house coverage; so the signal in the back of your house remains strong. It does this by creating a mesh network.

Popular Alternatives

- Eero Mesh WiFi (approx. $249) - Mesh networking was partially pioneered by Eero. Eero was recently acquired by Amazon, and their system works great with Alexa; if you want a Wi-Fi system in that ecosystem then this is your best option.

What You Need To Know

All of the products here work in the Nest app...except Nest Wifi; despite its name, you don't use the "Nest" app to use Nest Wifi; you use the Google Home app.

Installation

Self-guided and easy to do on your own.

Specs

I'm going to walk you through setting up both a router and mesh access point. You might not need both! Depending on your home, you might be fine with just a router.

According to Google, these are the recommendations for when you need an access point, and how large it should be:

Up to 2,200 SF - Just the router
Up to 3,800 SF - Router and access point
Up to 5,400 SF - Router and 2 access points
Each additional 1,600 SF - one access point per 1,600 SF

Unboxing

The router and access point don't look too different from each other. The access point is a little smaller and doesn't have any inputs (aside from power); the access point also has a speaker on the bottom—that's because the access point doubles as a Google speaker. So, you can ask it questions just as you would a Nest Mini speaker.

86 | *Google Your Home*

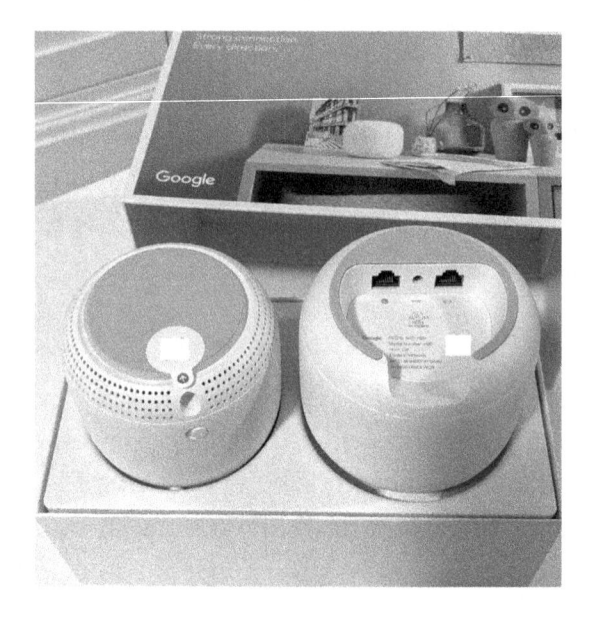

Below the devices is a very brief getting started guide.

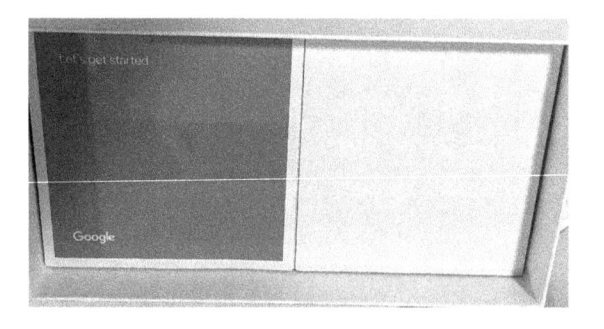

And below this are the power and network cables that you'll need to get things set up.

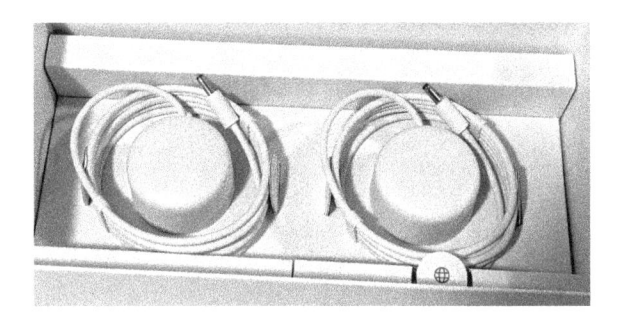

The Setup

Once you have it all up, you are ready to begin the setup. Remember, you will be setting this up in the Google Home app (not the Nest app). Personally, I found this to be a little confusing—it's called Nest Wifi, so I naturally went into the Nest app to set it up.

To get started, plug in your router near your Internet modem (if you are setting up an access point as well, leave it unplugged).

Once you open the Google Home app, you'll tap the + button in the upper left corner.

88 | *Google Your Home*

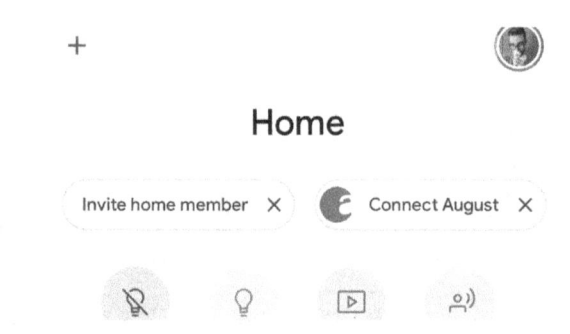

This will bring up the set up screen, which will ask you how you want to set it up. You'll want the first option.

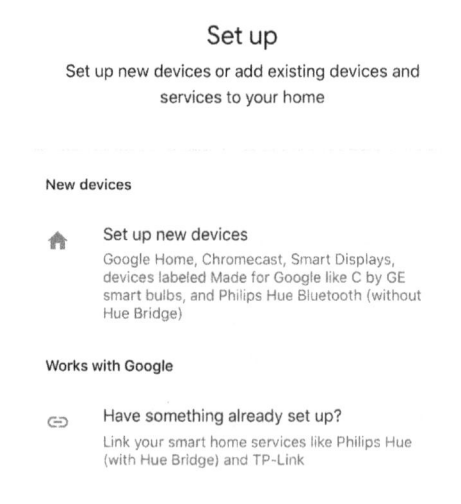

If you have never used the Google Home app, then you'll need to create a home here. If you have a Nest Mini, Google Home or other Google smart device, then you probably already have it set up. Just tap on the name of your Home.

Choose a home

You'll be able to control the devices and services in this home.

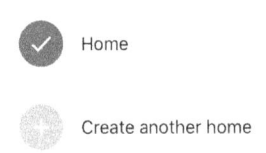

✓ Home

⊕ Create another home

It will automatically start looking for your device after you tap the next button.

Looking for devices

Once it finds it, you'll see a list of nearby devices; assuming this is the only new device you have plugged in, then you should see it listed as a Nest Wifi router.

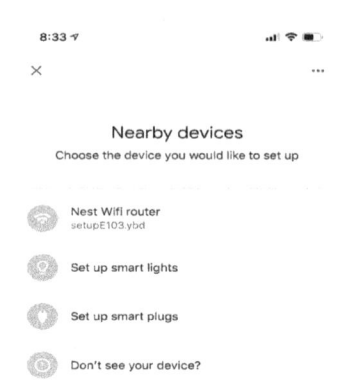

[Screenshot: Nearby devices screen showing Nest Wifi router (setupE103.ybd), Set up smart lights, Set up smart plugs, Don't see your device?]

At this point, it's going to ask for permission to use your mobile device's camera. Why? There's a QR device on the router. You'll have to scan that with your camera to complete the setup.

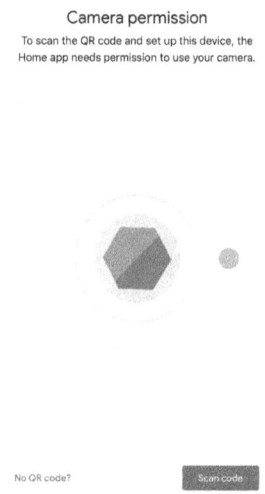

[Screenshot: Camera permission screen — "To scan the QR code and set up this device, the Home app needs permission to use your camera." with "No QR code?" and "Scan code" buttons]

Once it's scanned, it's going to ask permission to join your wireless network.

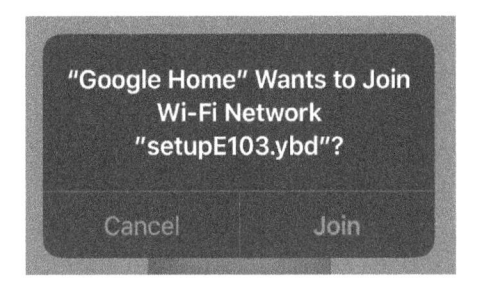

> "Google Home" Wants to Join Wi-Fi Network "setupE103.ybd"?
>
> Cancel   Join

At this point, you can connect your router into your modem. There are two ethernet network cable connections. Make sure you are using the one highlighted in the illustration.

Plug in WAN
The ethernet cable doesn't seem to be plugged into the WAN port properly

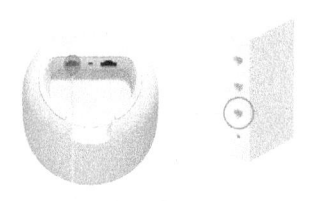

Next, you'll need to reboot your modem.

Reboot your modem
1) Unplug your Nest router and modem completely
2) Plug your modem back in and wait 1 minute
3) Plug your Nest router back in and wait 2 minutes. Then continue with setup

After the reboot you should be connected.
Connected

If there's a problem, you'll see a screen asking you to try again; personally, I ran into this the first time I set up the router and had to reset my modem and start over before it would work.

Problem connecting

Please check if you're online

Try again

Once you are connected, you'll be asked to name your network. You don't have to be technical here; you can name it "My_Awesome_Sauce_WiFi" or anything else (notice the underscores? There are a few rules to names—the biggest is you can't use spaces; use underscores to act as spaces)! Just remember, this is what people see when they come to your house and say, "Hey, what's your Wi-Fi?" so you might not to use something "Feet_Smell_Lover"! You'll be able to change this later—you'll also be able to create a guest network and family network.

Create a Wi-Fi name

Network name

Once your network name is picked, there's a handful of questions it will ask you. The first is if you want to send crash reports and stats to Google to help them improve the device; this is all done in the background and you don't notice it happening.

Turn on Wifi router and point usage stats?

Automatically send anonymous Wi-Fi feature related usage statistics and crash reports from all Wifi devices in your Wi-Fi network to Google in order to improve Google's Wifi products. This setting applies as you add or remove Wifi devices to this network. Learn more

You can turn this off any time in your network settings

No Thanks   Yes, I'm In

The next question is if you want cloud services turned on.

Turn on Nest Wifi cloud services?

Services and your privacy
Nest Wifi can store and analyze data about your entire network and devices to provide peak performance, historical network insights, and help when you need it. This setting applies as you add or remove Wifi devices to this network. Learn more

You can turn this off any time in your network settings.

Guest info
When guests use your Wi-Fi network, let them know that some of their info (such as IP and MAC addresses and usage data) can be seen through the Home app and is associated with your home and account.

No Thanks   Yes, I'm in

Once you answer the questions, you will be asked where the device is. If you select living room, but it's really in the bathroom it won't really mess anything up—it just helps you keep all your devices organized.

96 | *Google Your Home*

Where is this device?
Choose a location for your Wifi device. This will help you organize your devices.

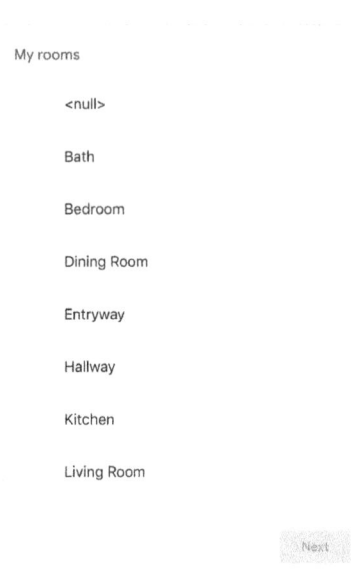

My rooms

<null>

Bath

Bedroom

Dining Room

Entryway

Hallway

Kitchen

Living Room

Next

Next it will create your Wi-Fi network.

Creating your Wi-Fi network...
Just a bit longer

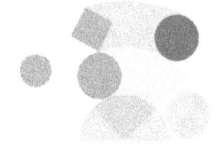

This step will take a few minutes and you'll probably see a second message.

Waiting for the final bits of setup to complete

Access Point

At this point in the setup, you'll be asked if you want to place an access point; if you have one, tap next; if you don't just tap Not Now. If you decide to buy an access point later, then you'll just run the set up again—if you've already have a Nest Wifi set up, it will recognize it and only set up the access point (not the router).

If you are doing this part of the setup, make sure you plug in your access point.

Place your next Wifi point

Wifi points work best when they're no more than two rooms away from each other or the Wifi router.

To use the Assistant, put the Wifi point in a place where you can easily talk to it.

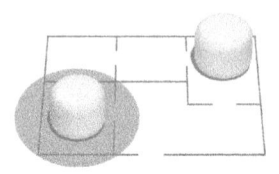

Not Now   Next

You'll get a few messages about looking for the device and preparing the device, but there won't be actions aside from tapping the occasional Next button.

Preparing mesh...

Just like the router, you'll have to scan the QR code to complete the setup.

Once you scan it, it will ask if you hear a sound. If you don't, you'll need to try again until you do.

Once more you'll be asked about the location of the device.

Finally, you'll have to wait a few minutes for things to be set up.

Waiting for the final bits of setup to complete

Remember I mentioned the speakers on the access point? The next part of the setup is about that. It will walk you through setting up Google Assistant.

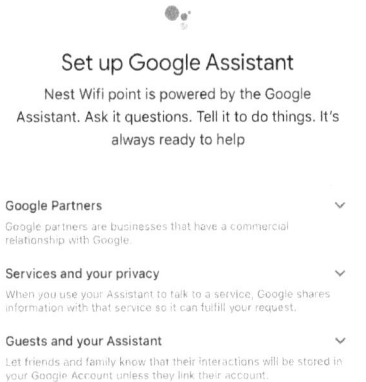

Set up Google Assistant

Nest Wifi point is powered by the Google Assistant. Ask it questions. Tell it to do things. It's always ready to help

Google Partners
Google partners are businesses that have a commercial relationship with Google.

Services and your privacy
When you use your Assistant to talk to a service, Google shares information with that service so it can fulfill your request.

Guests and your Assistant
Let friends and family know that their interactions will be stored in your Google Account unless they link their account.

Some of the next steps can be skipped. For example, the device can recognize voices—so if you have multiple people in your house, it will know when you are speaking versus someone else.

> **Teach your Assistant to recognize your voice**
>
> Voice Match helps your Google Assistant identify your voice on your Assistant devices, and tell you apart from others.
>
> No thanks   I agree >

You can also link the device to different music services, so when you ask Google to play a song, it will use the service to play it.

Link music services

Let everyone listen to your music just by asking the Assistant

Learn more

Sponsored

- YouTube Music — Free service available
- Google Play Music — Free service available
- Spotify — Spotify free service active ✓
- Pandora — Free radio service available
- Deezer — Deezer Premium+ account required

Not Now   Next

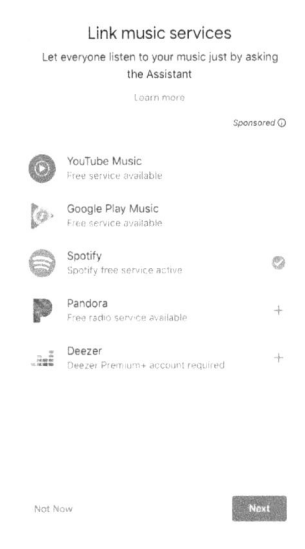

Finally, you have the option to use the device to make phone calls.

Get started with voice calls

Use your existing Google Duo account for high quality voice calls with anyone who has Duo. You can also call your own speaker to talk to people at home.

You can remove your Duo account from your speaker or delete your Duo account anytime in Assistant settings.

Not Now   Continue

Once Google Assistant is set up, it will begin testing your mesh connection.

Testing mesh connection
Checking the connection between your Wifi points

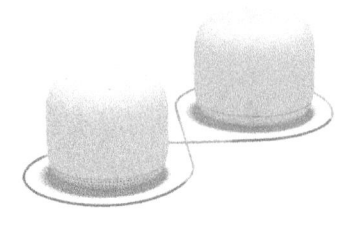

Assuming your mesh was set up correctly and in a good location, you'll get a message saying the connection is great.

Your mesh connection is great

Kitchen Wifi
Nest Wifi point   Great connection

Google will ask you next if you'd like to get emails about new features and services; it's completely optional.

Finally, your device will restart and also look for updates.

Once it reboots, you'll be all set! You can go to any computer or mobile device and the new Wi-Fi network should show up.

Your Nest Wifi is ready
Here's a review of what you have set up

Managing Nest Wifi

Now that everything is set up you can use your new network. But don't stop there! Now that it's set up, you can create guest networks, set up filters, family networks, and more!

To get started, open the Google Home app.

Once you are in the app, you will see icons for all the devices you can manage. The one you want here is "Wi-Fi".

The next screen will give you an overview of all your network settings (and by network, I mean the wireless network your Nest Wifi is connected to—you can manage your service provider settings here). You will also see the last tested network speed. If you think the Internet is slow, you can tap Run speed test to see the current speed.

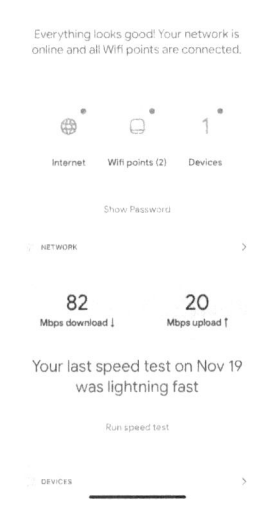

A speed test will take a minute or two.

Testing download speed...

When it's done, you will see your download and upload speed.

Your Internet speed
Lightning fast

86 ↓ Mbps download

20 ↑ Mbps upload

You can also see what devices are connected to your network by tapping on Devices. Remember these are the devices connected to your Nest Wifi—you may have other devices on your home network (such as plugged in directly to your modem with a network cable).

Internet   Wifi points (2)   Devices

Show Password

Tapping the Show Password button will show you what your network password is and also give you the option to copy it, text message it, or email it—so if someone says "hey, what's your Wi-Fi password?" You can message it to them.

PRIMARY NETWORK

Copy Message Email

Below this screen, you'll see connected devices and also see an option to set up a priority device. When you do this, it will ask how long you want the device to be a priority. Why would you want to do this? If you have several devices connected and one (such as a media device) will need more speed,

110 | *Google Your Home*

then you can set it up as the priority to ensure it gets the fastest connection.

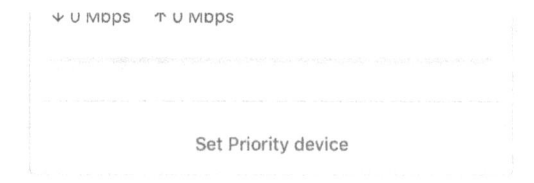

↓ 0 Mbps   ↑ 0 Mbps

Set Priority device

In the upper right corner is a config button.

When you tap on that, you'll be able to change your network name and password.

Primary Network

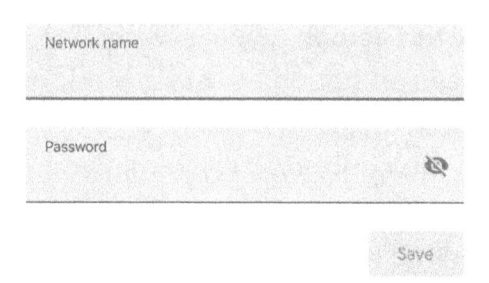

Network name

Password

Save

Below this, there are options to set up Family Wi-Fi and Guest Network; I'll cover this in a second; under this are options for Gaming preferred (if you stream games) and WPA3 (an extra layer for security). Finally, there's an option to factory reset your network.

Gaming preferred
Optimize Stadia gaming traffic, when active and available in your region. Learn more

WPA3
Use WPA3 security

Advanced networking
DNS, WAN, LAN, UPnP

Open source licenses

Restart network

Factory reset network

When you tap Family Wi-Fi, you'll be able to set up a network that blocks certain devices from using the Internet at certain times. To use it, tap Get started at the bottom.

112 | *Google Your Home*

Family Wi-Fi

Say goodbye to online distractions. Set a schedule to pause Wi-Fi on your kids' devices at bedtime, or pause Wi-Fi in the moment via the app or the Assistant, and block adult sites on any device.

Schedule a Wi-Fi pause
Set a schedule to automatically pause one or more groups at a preset time and day

Group your devices
Create a group of devices you would like to control at the same time

Get started

The first thing it will ask is to name the group; you can have several groups, so make the name distinctive.

Name your group
Try something like "Kids' devices"

Group name

Next, you'll see a list of devices that have connected to your network and you can pick which ones will be set up on this family plan.

Choose devices
Choose which devices you want in the group.

Next there's an option to block adult websites; it's just a toggle switch. It's a nice feature, but if you are concerned with child filtering, then you might consider dedicated software for filtering that has more options. No filter is perfect, however.

Restrict access
Turn on SafeSearch to automatically block millions of websites with adult content. Keep in mind that no filter can block every inappropriate site.

Kids

You will now get to pick when you want to pause the Internet on these devices. Remember they will still work—so they can still play games on the device if no Internet is required.

Schedule pauses
Schedule the devices in your groups to pause automatically whenever you want without lifting a finger

Not Now   Next

It will ask you to name your schedule. You can pick any name you want, but if you will have multiple schedules then make it descriptive so you remember what the schedule is for.

Name your schedule
Try something like Bedtime or Homework time

Bedtime, Homework, etc

Next

Next you'll be asked what group will be on the schedule. At this point, you'll only have one group.

Apply to a group
You can apply this schedule to a group and its devices

☐ Kids

Next

Finally, you'll be asked to set the time for the schedule.

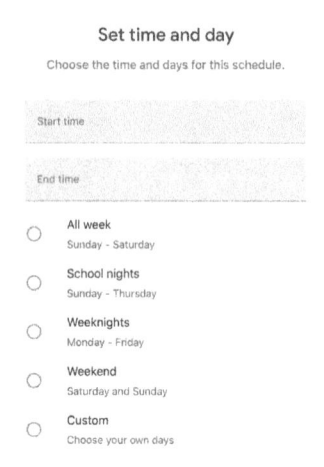

Set time and day

Choose the time and days for this schedule.

Start time

End time

○ All week
Sunday - Saturday

○ School nights
Sunday - Thursday

○ Weeknights
Monday - Friday

○ Weekend
Saturday and Sunday

○ Custom
Choose your own days

Once you add it, your schedule is all set and you'll see it under Family Wi-Fi.

Family Wi-Fi

Groups

Kids
1 device
Safesearch: OFF

✏️ Unpause

Schedules

Bedtime   ...
9:52 AM - 9:53 AM | School nights
Kids

To delete a group, tap the pencil under the group name.

Kids
1 device
Safesear

On the next screen, tap the three dots.

● ● ●

Finally, tap Delete Group.

🗑 Delete Group

❓ Help

💬 Feedback

✕ Cancel

Setting up a guest network is much quicker than a family one; just tap the network, then tap the Guest Network toggle.

Next, name your network.

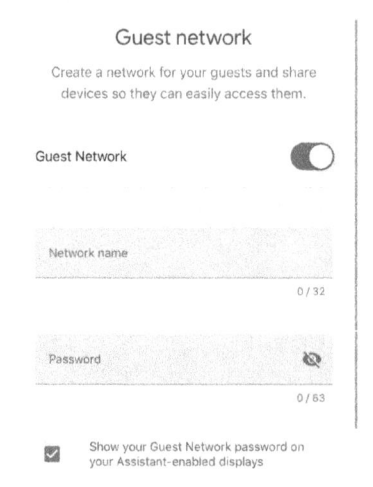

ABOUT THE AUTHOR

Scott La Counte is a librarian and writer. His first book, *Quiet, Please: Dispatches from a Public Librarian* (Da Capo 2008) was the editor's choice for the Chicago Tribune and a Discovery title for the Los Angeles Times; in 2011, he published the YA book The N00b Warriors, which became a #1 Amazon bestseller; his most recent book is *#OrganicJesus: Finding Your Way to an Unprocessed, GMO-Free Christianity* (Kregel 2016).

He has written dozens of best-selling how-to guides on tech products.

You can connect with him at ScottDouglas.org.

CPSIA information can be obtained
at www.ICGtesting.com
Printed in the USA
LVHW042032130120
643456LV00008B/1464/P